For you.
For Him.
And also for me.

Dear Reader,

Please enjoy this collection of experiences
in the form of poetry.

Several of these poems talk about heavy
issues such as addiction, abuse, self-harm,
assault, etc.

Not all of the experiences you will find in
these pages are my own. This book was
created to share and release healing
- mine and yours.

Here are the moments we are all exposed.

Samantha

Thank you,

to all those who have helped shape
me into who I am today. I wouldn't be
here without you.

Sam

Contents

Please note that the poems listed are the ones that have titles.

* poems with possible triggers

Half truths
Hidden between lines
Like a summer breeze that stirs the leaves
Ever so slightly
Guessing
What you meant to say

Half-finished
Thoughts and
Ideas and
Concepts but
Not quite done
Forgetting the most important part
Of
What I want to say

My hands ache
From all the things
I still hold onto
My heart still grieves
Every scar
Embedded in its core
They're begging me
To let go

I don't know what it's called
Only that I feel it

help

I know I'm the one
With my hands clamped over my ears
So tightly
To muffle the hate
And the words that cause me so much pain
That it muffles the love
And the words that would heal me too.
I know I'm the one
With tears in my eyes
Blurring my vision in such a way
I can no longer see clearly
But I don't know how to stop.

My Autistic Heart

Hug me
for I long to be squeezed
with
just enough gentle pressure
to feel safe
and loved
and enough
and -
stop. squeezing.
squishing.
too much pressure
suffocating
you are squeezing me wrong
I do not know how
or why
only that it is wrong
let me go
stop
STOP
you have squeezed too much
and now my heart
has
popped

There are so many things
To be angry about
So many things in the world
That need to be fixed
But I am just one person
and I am tired
from the things in my world
that I've had to fix.

Some moments
Are too soft for words
All we can do is be
And feel
And let it ache

Some moments
Are too harsh for words
All we can do is scream
And cry
And let it ache

Both moments
Leave us speechless
Taking our words
Replacing
With tears

To Nick

Hey.

How's it going? What's up with you?
You probably don't remember me.
After all,
you were high when we met.
But
I remember you.

I often see people out on the streets
and
I always think of you, Nick.
Where you are,
who you're with . . .
if you're still addicted
to meth,
cocaine,
cigarettes,
pot and heroin.

If

you're still struggling from injection to injection -
not really living;
barely surviving.

I wonder if you're still out there,
if you're even alive, Nick.
I wonder if your family worries
or if you even have a family.

I wonder if you've finally said yes
to help,
to Christ,
or if you're still roaming about
in darkness.

We only talked a bit
and
you weren't really coherent
but
you changed my life, Nick.

I told you about Jesus
and
you said you already knew.

What?

You knew,
oh Nick,
you already knew what to do
but you didn't want to.
Through your mumbling
you said
you weren't ready
for that kind of commitment.

How could you
choose
drugs
over freedom?

You knew the way out.
Why didn't you go?
You had all the help.
Why didn't you take it?
You understood.
Why didn't you try?

What is holding you back?

Nick, I don't understand!

It broke my heart
and
I cried that night.
And then I

I forgot.

I forgot on purpose.

I pushed you away, Nick.
I pushed you away because it was too painful to think of you
so lost,
addicted,
broken,
stumbling in the dark.

It hurt
that
the enemy had such a strong hold on your life
that

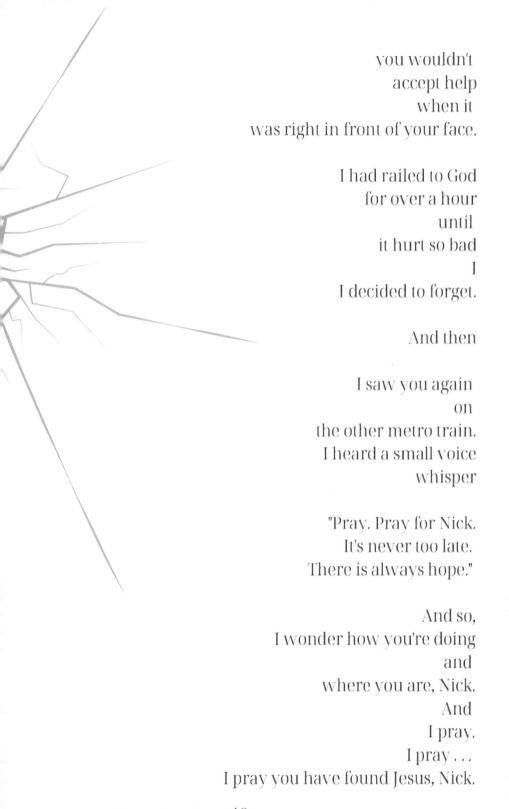

you wouldn't
accept help
when it
was right in front of your face.

I had railed to God
for over a hour
until
it hurt so bad
I
I decided to forget.

And then

I saw you again
on
the other metro train.
I heard a small voice
whisper

"Pray. Pray for Nick.
It's never too late.
There is always hope."

And so,
I wonder how you're doing
and
where you are, Nick.
And
I pray.
I pray . . .
I pray you have found Jesus, Nick.

addiction

Cold grip around my heart
And it *won't* let go
No rest
Until I do the thing I wish I wouldn't
Or
I don't do the thing I wish I would
Let go
I long to be free
To be me
Without this *thing*
And it's cold grip around my heart

Sometimes
It's too painful to hope

heavy
sleep with no rest
the world becomes more gray everyday
it tastes of ash
hopeless

Hope tastes like the first day of spring
as the snow begins to melt
It smells like the earth
after a late summer's rain
It feels like the sun
finally breaking through the clouds

Hope is the first breath
in a baby's lungs
their cry loud and piercing
Hope is a promise
of new beginnings
and never being alone

Hope is bursting forth
in glorious day
for He walked out of the grave
and He is walking still

Endless Love

Love
as boundless as the ocean
flowing,
as a river.
Remember it.

Love
as deep as the sea
high
as a mountain
True Love.

Let me listen to Your heartbeat
The steady pulse beneath my ears
Unchanging

Gently, please
Gently
If I give you my heart
Would you treat it gently?
My soul
Needs something gentle

Softly, please
Softly
Would you be soft with me?
With your voice and your words
Your touch
I need to be soft

Slowly, please
Slowly
If I say yes,
Can we dance slowly?
Our steps and movements
Let's go slow

Quietly, please
Quietly
Can we live quietly?
With souls bared and moments shared
Breathing peace
Let's be quiet

I miss you like the earth misses the sun when it rains
Knowing that to live and to grow
The absence is needed
Welcomed
In agony

Bold of you to assume I'm not already in love with you.

The Ways I Wish To Know You

Show me where you're broken
Not so I can fix you
But so I can be gentle when I brush against your cracks

Tell me of the deepness
Stirring inside your soul
The things you think no one would ever understand

Show me your happy place
The reasons you smile
Whatever it is that makes your heart overflow

Tell me all about
Your favorite memories
With full belly laughs and the good kind of tears

Show me all your laughter lines
Every scar upon your skin
Each story behind them

Tell me all the thoughts you think
When you lay awake at night
Unable to find rest

Show me all your quirks
Be wholly you
Without restraint

Tell me the truth
All the words
You're too afraid to say

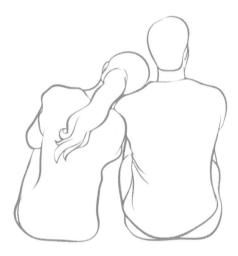

I don't have the words
to say everything
I wanna say
I just want to linger
in your presence
awhile longer

I Finally Understand

I have read many poems
by many great poets
that talk about love;
that talk about swooning and blushing and stuttering
and acting like a fool,
and I never really understood.
But then our eyes meet
across a crowded room
and the dimples on your cheeks deepen
and I think
I finally understand what they meant.

I wish we would say
Everything
That's been left
Unsaid
Aren't you curious, too?
But
Maybe there's a reason
It's left unsaid

If I believed in soulmates
I'd say that you were mine
Even if
I wasn't yours

And if I were honest with myself, I would admit just how much I care about him.

Sunflowers & Roses

Twenty-Seven roses
And I'm the only sunflower;
My wish to be a rose only grows with every hour.
Sunflowers are nice
But they aren't roses.
They lack the elegance
Grace
Poise
Of roses.
Every other girl seems to be
A rose;
Every other girl -
Except me:
The lonely sunflower.
Sunflowers are for Grandmas,
Aunts, mothers, sisters
And Roses -
Roses tell a girl you want to kiss her.

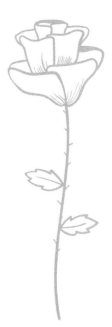

He has told her
too many times
that he only loves her
as a brother loves a sister
for him to tell her
he loves her more than that now.

And she has said
just the wrong thing
about loving him
too many times
to say they right thing now.

They are fools who do not know
how they love each other.

and suddenly
I realize
he looks at her
in a way
he's never looked at me

I hold myself back
because
I thought
that's what you wanted.
But sometimes
(when I turn and
find your eyes already on me
when your hands brush mine
purposely
when you smile
like we have a secret)
sometimes
I wonder
if maybe
- just *maybe* -
you do the same
for me.

I dream of your face
And my heart aches
For your smile, your gaze
To be directed my way
For the softness of falling in love
To be present in every touch
Every word
Every moment

And I can't help thinking
I should be with someone as broken as me
Forgetting
I am no longer broken
Just a little scarred

Stop *looking* at *me* like *that*
when we both know you don't mean it.

eventually

No one is alone forever
One day
eventually
Yet my Prince Charming hasn't shown up
And I don't know any knights in shining armor
Everyone tells me *eventually*
"Soon" - whatever that means
And usually
I'm fine with someday
With not yet, not now
But sometimes
eventually
Feels like a crumbled promise
fueled by unfulfilled dreams
and broken hearts
Some days
I'm tired of waiting

I know I was the one
Who walked the other way
But maybe
I wanted you to go after me
And give me a reason to stay

I keep trying
Hoping that maybe
Eventually
I'll get it right

The Only Reason

The only reason my teeth don't chatter
In the cold
Is because I clench them together

My tears don't fall
In the wind
Because I hold them hostage

My wounds don't bleed
In front of you
Because I've hand-stitched each one

The only reason my soul is silent
Is because you cut out its tongue

Upside Down

The world is upside down and so am I;
everything is different this way,
and yet, somehow, the same.
Footsteps in the hall make my heart race;
a pause, and I know what's coming.

Brace yourself.
(If I'm numb enough maybe it won't hurt.)

Stupid. Lazy. Incapable.
Furiously. Frustrated. FORTISSIMO.

I wonder why their words ring true
even when I know they're not.
I remain passive
- listless -
(It's better this way.)

Insults. Cursing. Harsh.
I am dumb.
Screeching words slice like razors. The same as when -
I say nothing.
(It doesn't matter anyway –)

Do they always have to yell?
Just because I don't respond
doesn't mean I can't hear.
The numbness has settled in
and now
it doesn't feel painful.
(It doesn't feel like anything.)

Biting. Sarcastic. Flippant.
Unworthy.
Selfish, ungrateful, immature -
My heart is bleeding
and it won't stop.
(I'm getting blood everywhere.)

I would say I'm sorry
but
apologies are just band aids on severed limbs;
you taught me that.
My mouth stays shut.

I know they're only words, angry and harsh,
but they cut like a knife through my muted stare.
Somehow, everything is the same, and yet,
this way is just different enough;
I am upside down and so is the world.

I know you didn't know
but that doesn't make it hurt any less

Peaches

Peaches remind me
Of summer
Of Georgia
Of the childhood
I never quite got
Biting into the plump fruit
Juices running down my chin
Takes me back to the days
Of messy hands
dirty faces
and sticky kisses anyways
Of running barefoot
through the grass
and playing in the creek -
watch out for snakes!

I thought that I was doing well

I thought that no one could ever tell

But

I tense up every time I shake hands with a man

I can't be alone even with my dad

I have panic attacks when I sit on the floor

I think that I hide it well

Until

My little brother asks me why

I don't let him hug me anymore

It's not your fault
they touched you like that.
Not saying no
still isn't a yes
and real love
doesn't leave bruises.

My Mother

When a girl
has a mother
who doesn't love herself,
you'd think
that maybe
she would learn how to hate her mother.

But no,
she doesn't.
She only learns
how to hate herself.

The Day He Left

I don't know what they were fighting about
Only that they were mad
I don't know when he packed
Only that he left
I don't remember what happened
Not really
Except
I stood in front of the door so he wouldn't leave
He told me to get out of the way or -
So I did
And then
He left

I don't know why he came back
Only that he did
But it didn't matter
Because
(Even though I was glad to have him back)
Every time they fought
I couldn't help but wonder
If this would be the time that he left and never came back
Or maybe she would

So I tried to be good
Always good
And maybe if I was always good
Or good enough
Neither one would leave me
But
As it turns out
I left before they could

Sometimes
I am still that scared little girl
Praying her daddy would come home
That her mom would stop being angry
That they would stop fighting
That someone
- anyone -
would rescue her from this mess she had made.
Sometimes
I am still afraid
to face
the things I know I must.
Some days
I am still her.

arms around me
but for a moment
and
it feels like coming home

Home smells like coffee
-dark and rich and fresh-
the kind of coffee that he brews

Home sounds like a late-summer afternoon
-bright and warm and happy-
because it's filled with her laughter

Home tastes like memories
-good and bad and in between-
it's always somebody's favorite meal.

Home feels like a thick blanket
-soft and calm and cozy-
because it's full of understanding.

Home looks like a dismal mood
-gray in the early morning hours-
but I finally see in color when you're around.

Things are good now
But they weren't always
And sometimes
I can't help that my defense mechanisms
Only push you away

Blood of Restoration

I am no stranger to blood
Skinned knees
Blistered heels
Scraped palms
and the bruises to go along with them
Sliced fingers
Nicked ankles
Womanhood
and the knowledge of what I've learned
Peeled lips
Chewed cuticles
Picked scabs
and the scars from where I -

I am no stranger to blood
Gashed foreheads
Bleed a lot
Sharp edges lead to scars
and staples hold more than just paper together

I am no stranger to blood
Sacrifice
Covering
Atonement
and the freedom from my torment

I am no stranger to blood
But this blood
- His blood -
is what restored me

Revival

Dead hearts beat once more
Match the pace of the Lord
It's time to be alive again

Breathe in healing
Renew the mind
Jesus reigns in us again

Fire roaring in our ears
Listen to the Spirit as He leads
The cry of the redeemed

Submerged in cleansing blood
Revive us again
The rhythm of life restored

Finding God

Once I heard a prophet say
If you don't know God
Look in the hands of tiny babes
And you will find Him there;
In the smallest flower,
The littlest bug on a blade of grass.
He is everywhere.

I found Him in the mountains -
On the shores of the sea.
In the eyes of wild deer
And tears of passing strangers;
Every place I looked,
He was there.

I can hear Him
In the laughter of children;
I can see Him
In every star of the night sky;
Each dip of the earth
Speaks of the One who created it.

Water soothes my wayward soul;
It calms the questions stirring inside
And leaves them for another day.
Music steadies my racing mind;
It laps against every wave of thought
As I gently drift away.
Nature stuns my scarred heart;
It silences the wounds of my past
And knows what I meant to say.

Songbird

Is a songbird
Still a songbird
If no one hears it sing?

If a skylark
Were to keep
Its music to itself
If a starling
Silenced
Its warbling tune
If a nightingale
Never sang
Its haunting melody

Is a songbird
Still a songbird
If no one hears it sing?

Contentment

golden light dancing across my eyelids
gentle breezes stirring the leaves on the trees
warmth upon my skin; heat without the bite
bonfire smoke in the crisp autumn air
my nose stinging with fresh cut grass and old books
home-made pie heaven to my tongue
splashing water and laughter in sweltering weather
good music and friendly conversation deep and light
flowers once more in bloom
bright stars galaxies away winking back at me
my soul finally at rest

Social Commentary

Too much
Yet not enough
Somehow
I'm always wrong.

Cracker girl -
I thought we were past judging the colors of our skin.
Left wing
Right wing
Shunned by both.

Too soft
Too pleasant
Take a stand -
but only if it's yours.
Say no -
but not to you.
Why is right on time
Considered late?

Too fake
Too poised
Smiles that don't
Reach eyes.
Try authenticity -
but only if it's not messy.
That's too real.

"Pretty face"
- eyes, nose, mouth -
Lumpy body
Bumpy skin
Assets.
Short but
Not that short -
I can never seem to fit any of the molds.

Unique but
Not really.
Just another sound
In the cacophony
Of opinions.

Accept
Except when -
We're all hypocrites.
No one takes accountability
- *responsibility* -
and acceptance doesn't mean approval.

It's less about what is right
or kind
And more about control -
I've learned the hard way.

Too much
Yet not enough
Somehow.
Finally, I no longer care.

A Pity

We're all so desperate to be understood,
We forget to be understanding.
"Are you listening?" she says
Not with her words but her gaze
The way she stares
How her eyes are searching
Unperturbed, unfazed
"Are you listening?"

We all so want to be heard,
We forget what it is to hear.
"Listen to me!" he shouts
Not with his words but his actions
How he draws attention
The way he pouts
Immature, Unrelenting
"Listen to me!"

We're all so obsessed with knowing,
We forget how to be known.
"We know!" we sigh
Not with our words but our attitudes
Thinking we're clever
Not realizing
We are very much alone
"We know!"

We're all so desperate to be understood,
We forget to be understanding.
We all so want to be heard,
We forget what it is to hear.
We're all so obsessed with knowing,
We forget how to be known.

And so
We end up alone.

A pity.

a soul without

a
soul
in which
nothing is kept
but everything
even love
is lost
is
a soul
in which
loneliness lives
there it thrives
that soul
i pity
oh
i will
forever
have pity on
that poor soul
for it exists
without
love

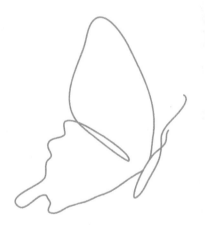

Perfect.
Control. Slipping.
Each. Movement. Measured.
If you aren't going to do it right, don't do it at all. Let someone else.
Did you realize
these were the words
that would destroy me?

Freedom is an open door;
step out into the sunlight
and leave those shackles behind

Freedom is brokenness restored;
let laughter bubble out
as scars begin to fade

Freedom is letting go -
hands finally open
lifted in surrender and praise

Freedom is floating into the atmosphere -
no longer held down by weight
that was never mine to begin with

the only one
who demands perfection
is yourself

dichotomy

I want to be skinny
Well, thinner, anyway
And taller
But also sometimes shorter

I want to say yes
I want to say no
I want to go
Away for a while

I want her to like me
and be my best friend
I want him to love me
the way I pretend I don't

I want to be organized
To never worry about money:
Forgetting bills
If I have enough

I want to feel safe, secure
I want to feel loved
I want to be famous
I want to be obscure
I want to be praised
I want to be hidden

I want guys
to ask me out just so I can say no

I want to be kissed
Passionately
in the pouring rain
(And *no*, not like the movies, but also *yes*, like the movies)

I want to eat food
And not gain weight

I want my worth to stop being determined by my weight
Or height
Or beauty
Or job
Or relationships.

I want to be confident
I want to commit
And stop being afraid of taking risks

I want to love well
I want children
Mine whether biological or not

I want a hug
A nap
A snack
I want to leave and not come back.

Sometimes
Not always
I want these things

But mostly
I want You and what You want.

I like who I get to be when I'm around you

I feel in color

Thoughts swirling like sunlight refracting on glass

I see in rhythm

Every item a part of some sort of dance

I hear in touch

Tone conveying more than any word could

I sing in harmony

Because my voice struggles with the melody

I think in sound

Words and pictures alike growing loud then soft again

Just because we feel
doesn't mean
what we say
isn't important

Anger can be hot and wet
Fierce
Burning
Fiery tears pour down flushed cheeks
Scalding
Blazing
Anger can be cold and dry
Freezing
Stoic
Harsh words spilling from numb lips
Brittle
Stinging
Each one just as destructive as the other

bouncing leg
chewed fingernails
picked lips
hair twirls
ear tugs
heart pounding
sweat pouring
thoughts racing
I swear I was fine just a second ago

Breathe
Pray, worship
repeat the verse again
Listen to *this* song
why isn't it working

Release
Surrender
Lock eyes on Him
Let go of what you're holding onto
It's hard to grab ahold of peace if your hands are already full

Finally still
and now
I know

Wrapped in blankets
still freezing;
it's hard to stay warm
when it's your soul that's cold.

Reaching out again
fingers barely brushing;
all that's left
is another unanswered text.

Designed for community
yet reality contains
empty tables
and lonely meals eaten in silence.

Sometimes, you don't get a chance to say goodbye.

Guard your heart
Hold your breath
Keep it all close to your chest
Until you choke on the words
You never got to say

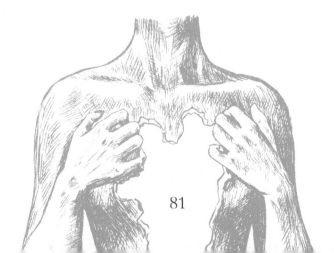

Words are just
words;
aren't they?
Then why
do so many of them
pierce my soul
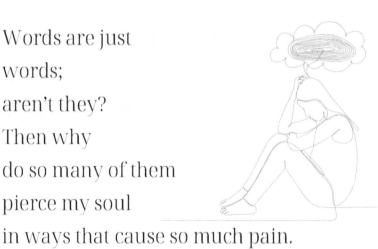
in ways that cause so much pain.

Why are you silent?
There is no guard at the door
Nothing holding your mouth shut
Except for uncertainty
And whatever's leftover from people pleasing
Why don't you speak?
You possess the words
And the confidence
Bold and sure
There is nothing wrong with your voice
Why are you silent?

This Is Religion

(as a young girl)

Sit. Down.
Stand up. For heaven's sake, don't slouch.
Look nice.
Smile.
Now. Be quiet.
(*And maybe you'll be good enough.*)

Kneel.
Bow your head.
In church, at the temple, during 5-in-the-morning prayer.
Before you go to bed
Pray.
Always pray.
In the morning, in the night;
before every meal is right;
5 times a day
pray.
(*Hopefully one day He'll listen.*)

Give.
Give your money
your time
your things
your life
to this -
It's the right way.
Wouldn't want to mess it up.
Give, give, give.
(*And maybe you'll be good enough.*)

Rules.
So many rules.
Don't swear or drink or dance or kiss.
No boys.
Don't look at or talk to or smile at or touch
boys.
Don't be friends with them.
But you must marry one
when you're older.
Be nice.
Don't lead them on.
And don't play games with
boys.
It's polite to say yes.
It's your fault he did that.
No one wants to marry someone
who is no longer clean.
You can only be happy if you're miserable.)

Don't.
Don't be aggressive or strong or tough.
Don't want or need or think or speak.
No questions.
Don't be stupid.
Do.
Do listen and sit and smile.
Do work and serve and help.
Do what they tell you.
Be modest and gentle.
Respect your elders.
Be good, pure, and kind.
So much pressure.
Don't, don't, don't.
Do, do, do.
(And maybe you'll be good enough.)

Sit *down*!
What are you doing?
Wait until after.
This is important.
(*And you are not.*)

Shut *up*!
Why are you talking?
Hold your tongue.
Listen to the reverend
the priest
the imam
the rabbi
he knows what he's saying.
His words are valuable.
(*And yours are not.*)

What are you *wearing*?
That's too much skin;
make sure you cover up.
What is on your face?
Makeup is for -
well, not you.
You should dye your hair
but not like that.
Why do you look so tired
and different?
Everything about you
Is wrong.
(*Looks like you'll never be good enough.*)

Is this really what God is like?

I will never be good enough
quiet enough
docile enough.
I will never serve enough
pray enough
give enough.

Running. Away.
From brokenness
worthlessness
silence, hypocrisy, selfishness.
From being too much.
From never being good enough.

Running. To.
Open arms
healthy community
forgiveness, healing, grace.
To finally feeling worthy.
To righteousness, holiness, truth.
To authentic love.

To Jesus.

This is so much different than I thought.
God is so much different than I thought.

I didn't find God until I left religion.

It is so hard
To feel beautiful
In a world
That constantly tells you that you're not

Just because we know it's a lie
doesn't make us believe it any less

don't you know
that women
are made of pain?
if you knew
how much pain I live with
you would know this truth
don't you know
that women
are made of beauty?
but the world
has caused them
to hide it away
don't you know
that women
are made of valor?
but our culture
has instilled
fear to cover it
don't you know
that women
are made of romance?
but we have lied
to each other
for so long
we are blinded to the truth

Can someone please explain
exactly *what* is *wrong*
with *other girls?*
Because I thought
we were all simply
human.

Inconvenient
Burden
Who told you these lies you believe about yourself?
Useless
Worthless
Stop letting others' words determine your value

I wish you could see
yourself
the way I see you

You are worth too much
to be anyone's second choice

And yet again
I find myself filled with hatred
But only towards
the choices I've made
and
who I've allowed
myself to become

Sometimes
I just need someone
To tell me
I'm enough

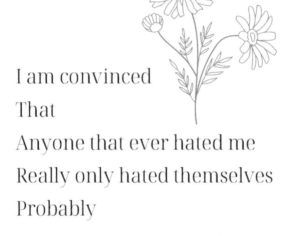

I am convinced
That
Anyone that ever hated me
Really only hated themselves
Probably

One day you will look at
yourself
And wonder
How you ever managed to hate
This vessel you came in

These hands were made for hard work and gentle touches;
these arms for hugs that heal and sharing loads.
These legs are meant to carry this soul a hundred thousand miles -
these feet are for dancing to every tune that calls.
These hips were made to rest a child on,
this back to stand straight and firm in times of trial.
These eyes were made to behold beauty . . .
these lips to bring Him glory forever.

And all the rest of me, too -
the parts I like and the parts I don't
are mine to care for
and mine to use for Him.

He didn't push Judas away
And He won't push you away.

I am worthy
not because of my jokes
or writing
or how I do my hair.

It's not because of my family
or clothes
or whether or not my bed is made.

Not even because of who I let speak into my life
or how much I serve
or give away.

No, I am worthy
because the Worthy One
says I am
and finally,
I believe it.

About The Author

Samantha is a recovering people pleaser who has been writing since she was 11 years old. Breath Exposed is her first printed publication. In addition to writing, Samantha loves Jesus, warm drinks on cold days, and the Oxford comma. She currently serves as her church's Kids Ministry Director in North Western Wisconsin. The oldest of 5, she often draws on experiences within her community in her writing. She hopes this work has brought healing and restoration to your life.

Made in the USA
Las Vegas, NV
02 August 2023

75546805R00059